anythink

Behind the Wheel of an
INDY CAR

BY ALEX MONNIG

Published by The Child's World®
1980 Lookout Drive • Mankato, MN 56003-1705
800-599-READ • www.childsworld.com

Acknowledgments
The Child's World®: Mary Berendes, Publishing Director
Red Line Editorial: Design, editorial direction, and production
Photographs ©: Will Lester/AP Images, cover, 1; Nam Y. Huh/AP Images, 4;
Hodag Media/Shutterstock Images, 7, 14, 18, 21; Shutterstock Images, 8;
Michael Kim/Corbis, 11; Action Sports Photography/Shutterstock Images, 13;
Michael Krinke/iStockphoto, 17

ISBN 9781634074346

LCCN 2015946231

Printed in the United States of America
Mankato, MN
December, 2015
PA02282

Table of
CONTENTS

Chapter 1

IN THE INDY 500

The Indianapolis 500 is one of the biggest Indy car races in the world. And you are in the middle of it. You have earned your way here after years of racing. Your team has decided you are the driver who can bring home the title. But to do so, you will have to beat a field full of great racers from around the world.

You are on lap 150 of 200. You and your competitors are cruising at about 220 miles per hour (354 km/h). You and a number of others are bunched in a close group ahead of the main pack.

It takes extra awareness to stay in a race like this one. With so many cars whipping around the track in a blur, even the tiniest mistake can lead to disaster. It is not only the race that could be lost. Lives could be lost, too.

Your yellow car sticks out among the red and white vehicles surrounding you. You are not a driver who takes unnecessary risks. But all successful drivers have to take some chances. With drivers

◄ Huge crowds gather to see popular Indy car races, such as the Indianapolis 500.

speeding around so quickly and closely, just getting behind the wheel of an Indy car is a risk.

Some of the other drivers are willing to push the limits of safety. No drivers want to injure other racers. But everybody is looking for every possible edge over the rest of the racers. That means driving as closely as possible when drafting. It also means banking efficiently on turns.

A driver in a red car closes in on you. He is one of the best in the world. He is also known for taking risks. You pull ahead of the pack by a slight margin. The red car stays right behind you.

You cannot believe how close he is. He somehow continues getting closer. Your hands tighten a bit around the steering wheel.

THE INDIANAPOLIS 500

The Indianapolis 500 takes place every year at Indianapolis Motor Speedway in Indiana. The first Indy 500 took place on May 30, 1911. Ray Harroun won the race that day. Since then, three drivers have won the race a record four times: A. J. Foyt, Al Unser, and Rick Mears. Winners are awarded the Borg-Warner Trophy. It is tradition to drink milk in victory lane to cool off after the long, hot race.

You start to get nervous. He goes to the inner edge of the turn. His car slowly drifts closer to yours. Then you feel it. His car's wheels touch yours. You start to lose control.

▲ Indy cars have exposed wheels that stick out from the cars' bodies.

Chapter 2

SPEEDING TOWARD DANGER

Growing up, you spent years around Indy cars. You loved watching races. But you also loved the cars themselves. When you first saw an Indy car, you had no idea what to think. It looked very different from the other race cars you had seen. The main difference is that an Indy car is largely uncovered. There is no roof over the driver's seat. The car also sits very low to the ground.

You had to learn more about Indy car racing. From reading books, you learned that the long, narrow body of the car is called the **chassis**. It almost comes to a point in the front. The chassis holds many of the car's most important parts. It also contains the area where the driver sits. You read that the area around the chassis is called the **side pod**. This gives the car a wider look and holds other important parts.

◄ Indy cars sit low to the ground, and most chassis are about 40 inches (102 cm) tall.

You were surprised by how far the front wheels seemed to stick out of Indy cars. Rods extend from the chassis to hold the tires in place. The back tires are more covered. They also are much bigger than the front tires.

The Indy cars you saw on television had front and rear wings. The wings looked like large rectangular plates. Each car had one at the front tip of the car and another at the back of the car, behind the wheels. The race announcer explained that the wings create downward air pressure. This helps the cars stay balanced while they zoom around the track.

The Indy cars you saw on television traveled as fast as 235 mph (378 km/h). When your dad took you to see your first race, you realized just how fast that was. Standing at the finish line, you could not tell who won the race. The winner had finished just a fraction of a second faster than the next driver.

After the race, you knew you wanted to become a professional Indy car driver. But you understood that driving any vehicle at hundreds of miles per hour could be dangerous. Being safe was far more important than winning. So you learned all you could about the dangers of racing and how to be safe.

With cars traveling at such high speeds, Indy car races often ▶ come down to fractions of a second.

Crashing has been part of Indy car racing since its beginning. Cars and drivers have become safer over time. But the danger is still present. Drivers speed around tracks in tight packs. That means cars can spin after just a small bump.

Sometimes the results are tragic. One of the worst crashes happened during the 2011 Las Vegas Indy 300. It involved star driver Dan Wheldon. There was contact between some cars coming around a turn. They started losing control. Soon, 15 cars were involved. Car parts and flames shot out everywhere. Wheldon died in the crash.

DAN WHELDON

British driver Dan Wheldon was 33 when he died on October 16, 2011. He was one of the best drivers in the world. He had won that year's Indy 500. He also had won the race in 2005. His death shook the racing world. Drivers called the crash the worst they had ever seen.

If you were going to become a driver, you needed to know how to protect yourself. You found out that all drivers must wear helmets with microphones in them. These devices help the drivers communicate with their teams during races. Drivers also must use harness systems when racing to keep their heads from moving too much.

▲ Indy car star Dan Wheldon died in a bad accident during the Las Vegas Indy 300 on October 16, 2011.

There are rules about the clothing drivers must wear. All racers need a one-piece suit that is fire resistant. They also need to wear fire-resistant socks, gloves, and shoes. It seemed like drivers needed to wear a lot of safety equipment. But after seeing what could happen on the track, you understood why.

Chapter 3

RACE RULES

You knew there was much more to learn before you started racing. So you decided to go straight to the source. Fans have great access at many Indy car races. People are sometimes allowed to talk to members of the pit crews.

The next time there was an Indy car race near your town, you went down to the track to learn more. You got lucky. You ended up watching the race with one of the pit crews.

The first thing that confused you was the number of flags. The crews use a variety of flags to communicate with their drivers. Different flags tell the drivers different things. Members of the pit crew explained what each one meant.

That was just the start of your education. The members shared their deep racing knowledge with you all day. They taught you about different strategies used during races. One of the most important was drafting.

◄ Pit crews work to keep Indy cars in top shape throughout races.

You had seen drivers get close to other drivers during Indy races. The crew explained why they did this. In a race, all of the cars cut though the air as they go around the track. Some of the air goes over the cars. Some goes below. This creates pockets with no air resistance just behind the speeding cars. Getting close behind other cars helps the drivers cruise easier. The cars in front take on all the air resistance.

The crew explained that navigating banking turns was another key to winning. The angled track allows drivers to keep their speed up while turning. The fastest way through a banking turn is

FLAG COLORS

A green flag indicates the start of a race. A black-and-white checkered flag is waved at the end. Some like to say a driver has "taken the checkered flag" when he or she wins a race. The yellow flag is the caution flag. That means there are dangerous conditions on the course. This is usually due to a crash. Blue flags tell drivers who are far behind in the race that a faster car is attempting to pass. The driver of the slower car must move to let the faster car pass.

▲ Race officials use flags to communicate various messages to drivers.

to start high up near the wall and then come down the track out of the curve.

You saw firsthand how important quick pit stops are, too. Cars cannot handle a full race without maintenance. So drivers pull into their teams' pits to get important work done. Crews change tires and add fuel in seconds. The drivers then quickly return to racing on the course.

Chapter 4

SERIOUS SERIES

You worked hard over the years to become a strong driver. Luckily for you, a car company discovered you at a small race a few years ago. Now the company is your **sponsor**. It has helped you become one of the best drivers in the world. That has earned you a spot in some of the best racing series.

The two major racing series are the IndyCar Series and the Formula One series. The IndyCar Series takes place in the United States. Formula One races take place in various countries. You race in the IndyCar Series. You get points based on the place in which you finish. The person with the most points at the end of the year wins the series.

The Indy 500 is the most famous IndyCar Series race. Now you are in the middle of it, trying to fight off the red car. Your tires have just touched. You feel your car start to waver. You head up a banked turn to get yourself some space.

◀ **Drivers on the inside of a turn travel a shorter distance than those on the outside.**

Now the red car is in front of you. But you know what to do. You speed up to get behind him. You inch up closer and closer. You feel your car gliding easily. The drafting is working perfectly. This is right where you want to be.

Soon there are only 12 laps left. It is time to make your move. You want to catch your opponent off guard. If you wait too long to pass, the driver will be expecting it. So you decide to go now.

You go low coming out of the turn. He stays high. You pull up alongside the red car. And you come out of the turn ahead. You spend the rest of the race fighting for position. He slips in behind you to draft. But each time he tries to pass, you block him.

You both come around the last turn into the final straightaway. He pulls to your right and slowly inches up beside you. But you are still in the lead. You push the gas pedal to the floor and cross the finish line first. You hear your team celebrating in your headset. You have just won the most famous Indy car race in the world. But you could not have done it without your crew. You cruise into victory lane to join the celebration.

Winning racers head to victory lane to celebrate ▶ with their pit crews.

GLOSSARY

banking (BANGK-ing): In racing, banking means driving on turns that are angled instead of flat. Banking effectively is an important part of Indy car racing.

chassis (CHAS-ee): The chassis is the body of an Indy car, which holds the engine and driver's seat. The chassis of your car is painted bright yellow.

drafting (DRAFT-ing): Drafting is driving closely behind another car. Drafting allows drivers to take advantage of less air resistance.

harness (HAHR-nis): A harness is a system of straps and buckles that tightens to keep something in place. The harness in your driver's seat keeps your head from bouncing around while driving.

pit crews (pit krooz): Pit crews perform car maintenance during races. Pit crews replace tires and add gas in just a few seconds during competitions.

side pod (siyd pod): The side pod sits on both sides of the chassis. The side pod holds important car parts and protects the driver in case of a crash.

sponsor (SPON-ser): To sponsor a driver is to pay for someone to race. Your sponsor has allowed you to take part in big races.

TO LEARN MORE

Books

Arute, Jack. *Tales from the Indianapolis 500.* New York: Sports Publishing, 2012.

David, Jack. *Indy Cars.* Minneapolis, MN: Bellwether Media, 2008.

Kramer, Ralph. *The Indianapolis 500: A Century of Excitement.* Iola, WI: Krause Publications, 2010.

Web Sites

Visit our Web site for links about Indy cars: childsworld.com/links

Note to Parents, Teachers, and Librarians: We routinely verify our Web links to make sure they are safe and active sites. So encourage your readers to check them out!

SELECTED BIBLIOGRAPHY

Augustine, Bernie, and Teri Thompson. "Dan Wheldon Killed in 15-Car IndyCar Crash at Las Vegas 300." *Daily News.* NYDailyNews.com, 17 Oct. 2011. Web. 24 Jun. 2015.

"G Force Factor: 'Sport Science' Examines Banking." *IndyCar.com.* INDYCAR, 7 Jun. 2013. Web. 24 Jun. 2015.

"Indy 500 Traditions and FAQs." *The Racing Capital of the World.* IMS LLC, 2015. Web. 24 Jun. 2015

Leerhsen, Charles. "One Hundred Years of the Indy 500." *Smithsonian Magazine.* Smithsonian Institution, 2011. Web. 24 Jun. 2015.

INDEX

ABOUT THE AUTHOR

Alex Monnig is a freelance journalist from Saint Louis, Missouri, who now lives in Sydney, Australia. He graduated with his master's degree from the University of Missouri in 2010. During his career, he has spent time covering sporting events around the world.